essential Musicianship

for band

INTERMEDIATE

ensemble concepts

Eddie Green
John Benzer
David Bertman

Percussion by
Evelio Villarreal

ISBN 978-0-634-09466-8

HAL•LEONARD®
CORPORATION
7777 W. BLUEMOUND RD. P.O. BOX 13819 MILWAUKEE, WI 53213

From the Authors

Welcome to *Essential Musicianship for Band* and *Ensemble Concepts – Intermediate Level*.

This book is intended to support your current band method by helping to reinforce and expand the skills and knowledge of the developing musician. Based on years of individual practice by experienced musicians, the daily exercises in *Ensemble Concepts* have been adapted for an entire band. Focusing on listening skills and consistent fundamentals, these exercises will help lay the foundation to build an excellent ensemble and create a fulfilling musical experience.

The concepts used in this book are taught to all music education students at the University of Houston's Moores School of Music. Dr. David Ashley White, Director of the Moores School, and Dr. Lynn Lamkin, Associate Director, enthusiastically endorse the faculty's concept of ensemble training. Their commitment to the development of these future music educators is demonstrated by their continued involvement in this process.

How to Use *Ensemble Concepts*

The goal of *Ensemble Concepts* is to provide appropriate exercises for use at at every rehearsal. These may be used at any stage of ensemble development, including the beginner level. Basic performance skills are introduced individually and then combined for more challenging practice. While the concepts are presented in developmental order, the intent is not to proceed line by line, but rather to purposefully and consistently practice targeted skills until proficiency is achieved.

This book also includes information to assist the director in becoming a more proficient ensemble technician. However, it does not attempt to influence the director's personal sound concept, musical integrity or creativity.

Again, this book should not be followed in "line order." Use exercises from as many units as the students are ready to learn. It is also beneficial to practice exercises that reinforce the same skills used in the band's method book or performance music. This will help achieve a more unified and musically satisfying experience.

Each exercise includes goals for the students, as well as information for the director. Not all student goals should be attempted at the same time. One or two will suffice. Avoid proceeding to a new goal until all students are meeting current goals with competency.

Final thought:
Success with *Ensemble Concepts* will only be achieved through the director's proactive and reactive approach to the ensemble and the music.

The Exercises

Most often, the exercises should be performed with a metronome adjusted to accommodate the skill level of the band. For exercises with longer notes, the tempo can be increased if students lack sufficient air to complete the exercise. When faster rhythms occur, the tempo can be decreased.

Dynamics should not be applied to the exercises. Each should be played at a level that produces the students' most resonant sound.

Some lines are written in octaves to accommodate range issues. In certain exercises, alternate exercises (written down a perfect fourth) are included for the clarinet, bass clarinet and French horn to accommodate additional range problems.

Percussion

Percussion parts are included for all exercises. However, the director may choose not to include percussion in the daily exercises. In some cases, this allows the director to focus on important sound and ensemble refinements and then work with the percussion section separately.

Additional Materials

The back of this conductor's book contains additional information taken from *Ensemble Concepts – High School Level*. This information may help introduce and reinforce the many of the concepts and goals in this book. Sections on posture, breathing, articulation, balance and conducting are among the topics discussed.

Pulse and the Metronome

Pulse is a vital part of all music. In performance, maintaining a steady pulse is a necessary skill for any ensemble's success. The best ensembles are those who play with unified, internal "clock" that becomes the foundation for all the artistic and interpretive aspects of musicality.

Most beginning students cannot maintain a steady beat without some assistance. A metronome can serve as an ideal tool for instilling a sense of musical pulse in the developing musician. A metronome will not only establish and maintain a tempo but, with some models, also create subdivisions of the beat.

Most often, the exercises in *Ensemble Concepts* should practiced with a metronome placed for the entire band to hear. Put the metronome in different locations throughout the band (in the middle, side right, front left, etc.) challenging students to listen for the pulse. This will develop the students' aural sensitivity to where the pulse is located within the ensemble and more importantly, within the music itself.

Use this opportunity to walk around the room, listening from different perspectives, and encouraging the students to listen and "lock" to the steady beat. As students develop a sense of pulse, turn the metronome off and return to the podium, now encouraging the eyes to follow your conducting.

1. Ensemble Sound
1-1 Block Concert F

ⓂⓂ = Muffle (dampen)
*Xylophone, Bells, Marimba, Vibes
𝄢 (Vibes only)

Director Reminders
- Focus on the start and release of each note.
- Players should stay totally set during the rests, which are an active part of the phrase.
- A metronome will establish a steady pulse to help achieve all student goals.

Student Goals
1. Take a breath together before each note.
2. Start each note together and keep a steady air stream for four full beats.
3. Release (end) each note together.
4. During whole rests, breathe on count 3.
5. Vibrato-producing instruments may use vibrato.

Percussion Goals
1. Breathe together.
2. Start together.
3. Strike the instrument in the same place with the same energy every time.
4. All strokes should have a smooth beginning, middle and end.
5. Match the dynamic level of the wind players.

1-2 Matching Sections – Non-Touching Notes

 Director Reminders
- Focus on the start and release of each note.
- If the tubas/low woodwinds cannot model a resonant tone quality, another section can begin the exercise, and then return to the indicated order.
- A metronome will establish a steady pulse to help achieve all student goals.

Student Goals
1. Take a breath together before each note.
2. Start each note together and keep a steady air stream for four full beats.
3. Release (end) each note together.
4. Each instrument group should "match" their note to other groups.
5. Vibrato-producing instruments may use vibrato.

Percussion Goals ✔
1. Breathe together.
2. Start together.
3. Strike the instrument in the same place with the same energy every time.
4. All strokes should have a smooth beginning, middle and end.
5. Match the dynamic level of the wind players.

1-3 Matching Sections – Touching Notes

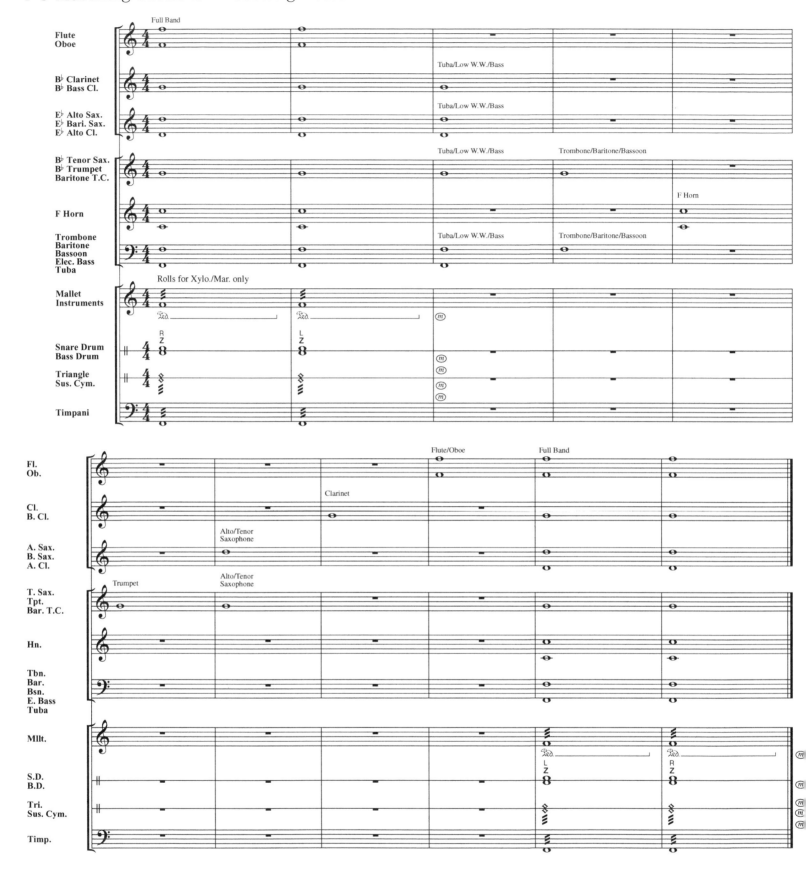

Director Reminders
• Focus on the start and release of each note.
• If the tubas/low woodwinds cannot model a resonant tone quality, another section can begin the exercise, and then return to the indicated order.
• A metronome will establish a steady pulse to help achieve all student goals.

Student Goals
1. Take a breath together before each note.
2. Start each note together and keep a steady air stream for four full beats.
3. Release (end) each note together.
4. Each instrument group should "match" their note to other groups.
5. Vibrato-producing instruments may use vibrato.

Percussion Goals
1. Breathe together.
2. Start together.
3. Strike the instrument in the same place with the same energy every time.
4. All strokes should have a smooth beginning, middle and end.
5. Match the dynamic level of the wind players.

2. Rhythm and Tonguing Exercises
2-1 Long to Short Notes

ⓜ = Muffle (dampen)
*Xylophone, Bells, Marimba, Vibes
🎵 (Vibes only)

Director Reminders
- Focus on the start and release of each note.
- Players should stay totally set during the rests, which are an active part of the phrase.
- A metronome will establish a steady pulse to help achieve all student goals.

Student Goals ✔
1. Breathe and start together.
2. The tongue should move up and down naturally; the same part of the tongue should go to the same spot with the same strength each time.
3. Match tonguing style (articulation).
4. Match note lengths.
5. Keep the air steady, constant and smooth.

Percussion Goals ✔
1. Breathe together.
2. Start together.
3. Strike the instrument in the same place with the same energy every time.
4. The quicker the notes, the smoother the mallet/stick motion should look.
5. Rolls should be smooth and even.

2-2 Short to Long Notes

Director Reminders

- Focus on the start and release of each note.
- Players should stay totally set during the rests, which are an active part of the phrase.
- A metronome will establish a steady pulse to help achieve all student goals.

Student Goals ✓

1. Breathe and start together.
2. The tongue should move up and down naturally; the same part of the tongue should go to the same spot with the same strength each time.
3. Match tonguing style (articulation).
4. Match note lengths.
5. Keep the air steady, constant and smooth.

Percussion Goals ✓

1. Breathe together.
2. Start together.
3. Strike the instrument in the same place with the same energy every time.
4. The quicker the notes, the smoother the mallet/stick motion should look.
5. Rolls should be smooth and even.

2-3 Long to Short Notes

Director Reminders

- Focus on the start and release of each note.
- Players should stay totally set during the rests, which are an active part of the phrase.
- A metronome will establish a steady pulse to help achieve all student goals.

Student Goals ✔

1. Breathe and start together.
2. The tongue should move up and down naturally; the same part of the tongue should go to the same spot with the same strength each time.
3. Match tonguing style (articulation).
4. Match note lengths.
5. Keep the air steady, constant and smooth.

Percussion Goals ✔

1. Breathe together.
2. Start together.
3. Strike the instrument in the same place with the same energy every time.
4. The quicker the notes, the smoother the mallet/stick motion should look.
5. Rolls should be smooth and even.

2-4 Long to Short Notes

Director Reminders
- Focus on the start and release of each note.
- Players should stay totally set during the rests, which are an active part of the phrase.
- A metronome will establish a steady pulse to help achieve all student goals.

Student Goals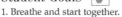
1. Breathe and start together.
2. The tongue should move up and down naturally; the same part of the tongue should go to the same spot with the same strength each time.
3. Match tonguing style (articulation).
4. Match note lengths.
5. Keep the air steady, constant and smooth.

Percussion Goals
1. Breathe together.
2. Start together.
3. Strike the instrument in the same place with the same energy every time.
4. The quicker the notes, the smoother the mallet/stick motion should look.
5. Rolls should be smooth and even.

2-5 Short to Long Notes

Director Reminders

- Focus on the start and release of each note.
- Players should stay totally set during the rests, which are an active part of the phrase.
- A metronome will establish a steady pulse to help achieve all student goals.

Student Goals

1. Breathe and start together.
2. The tongue should move up and down naturally; the same part of the tongue should go to the same spot with the same strength each time.
3. Match tonguing style (articulation).
4. Match note lengths.
5. Keep the air steady, constant and smooth.

Percussion Goals

1. Breathe together.
2. Start together.
3. Strike the instrument in the same place with the same energy every time.
4. The quicker the notes, the smoother the mallet/stick motion should look.
5. Rolls should be smooth and even.

3. Intervals Moving Down and Up

3-1 Intervals Down

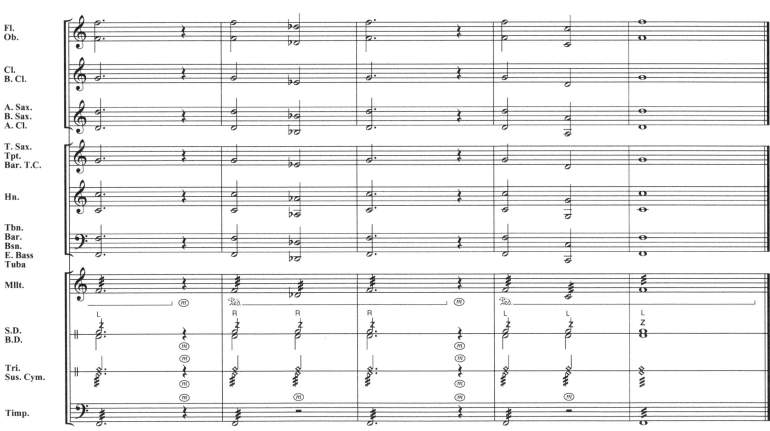

ⓜ = Muffle (dampen)
*Xylophone, Bells, Marimba, Vibes
🎹 (Vibes only)

Director Reminders

- Focus on the start and release of each note.
- Carefully listen to the concert Fs before and after each rest. They should sound exactly the same.
- All intervals should resonate with the same character.

Student Goals

1. Breathe together before the first note.
2. Match articulation.
3. Match note lengths.
4. Strive for a clear tone quality.
5. The wider the interval, the more focused the airstream should be.

Percussion Goals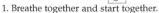

1. Breathe together and start together.
2. Posture should be natural with the body position balanced.
3. Strike the instrument in the same place with the same energy every time.
4. Match the dynamic level of the winds.
5. Rolls should be smooth and even.

3-2 Intervals Up

Director Reminders
- Focus on the start and release of each note.
- Carefully listen to the concert Fs before and after each rest. They should sound exactly the same.
- All intervals should resonate with the same character.

Student Goals
1. Breathe together before the first note.
2. Match articulation.
3. Match note lengths.
4. Strive for a clear tone quality.
5. The wider the interval, the more focused the airstream should be.

Percussion Goals
1. Breathe together and start together.
2. Posture should be natural with the body position balanced.
3. Strike the instrument in the same place with the same energy every time.
4. Match the dynamic level of the winds.
5. Rolls should be smooth and even.

3-3 Intervals Up and Down

Director Reminders
- Focus on the start and release of each note.
- Carefully listen to the concert Fs before and after each rest. They should sound exactly the same.
- All intervals should resonate with the same character.

Student Goals ✓
1. Breathe together before the first note.
2. Match articulation.
3. Match note lengths.
4. Strive for a clear tone quality.
5. The wider the interval, the more focused the airstream should be.

Percussion Goals ✓
1. Breathe together and start together.
2. Posture should be natural with the body position balanced.
3. Strike the instrument in the same place with the same energy every time.
4. Match the dynamic level of the winds.
5. Rolls should be smooth and even.

3-4 Intervals Up and Down (Model and Ensemble)

3-4 cont.

Director Reminders
- Focus on the start and release of each note.
- The ensemble should match all aspects of the model's performance.
- All intervals should resonate with the same character.

Student Goals ✓
1. Breathe together before the first note.
2. Match articulation.
3. Match note lengths.
4. Strive for a clear tone quality.
5. The wider the interval, the more focused the airstream should be.

Percussion Goals ✓
1. Breathe together and start together.
2. Posture should be natural with the body position balanced.
3. Strike the instrument in the same place with the same energy every time.
4. Match the dynamic level of the winds.
5. Rolls should be smooth and even.

4. Pick-up Exercises
4-1 Moving Up

4-2 Moving Up (2 notes)

🄼 = Muffle (dampen)

*Xylophone, Bells, Marimba, Vibes

𝄁 (Vibes only)

Goals for Exercises 4-1 and 4-2

Director Reminders
- Preparatory counts will be given by the conductor.
- All intervals should have the same resonance as concert F.
- A metronome will establish a steady pulse to help achieve all student goals.

Student Goals ✔
1. Breathe together before the first note.
2. Each pick-up note should strengthen to beat 1 (downbeat).
3. Match articulation.
4. Match note lengths.
5. The wider the interval, the more focused the airstream should be.

Percussion Goals ✔
1. Breathe together and start together.
2. Each pick-up note should strengthen to beat 1 (downbeat).
3. The quicker the notes, the smoother the mallet/stick motion should look.
4. Match the dynamic level of the winds.
5. Hands, wrists and arms should look natural and feel soft and relaxed.

4-3 Moving Up (3 notes)

4-4 Moving Down

Goals for Exercises 4-3 and 4-4

Director Reminders
- Preparatory counts will be given by the conductor.
- All intervals should have the same resonance as concert F.
- A metronome will establish a steady pulse to help achieve all student goals.

Student Goals ✓
1. Breathe together before the first note.
2. Each pick-up note should strengthen to beat 1 (downbeat).
3. Match articulation.
4. Match note lengths.
5. The wider the interval, the more focused the airstream should be.

Percussion Goals ✓
1. Breathe together and start together.
2. Each pick-up note should strengthen to beat 1 (downbeat).
3. The quicker the notes, the smoother the mallet/stick motion should look.
4. Match the dynamic level of the winds.
5. Hands, wrists and arms should look natural and feel soft and relaxed.

4-5 Moving Down (2 notes)

Timp. Tacet

4-6 Moving Down (3 notes)

Timp. Tacet

Goals for Exercises 4-5 and 4-6

Director Reminders
- Preparatory counts will be given by the conductor.
- All intervals should have the same resonance as concert F.
- A metronome will establish a steady pulse to help achieve all student goals.

Student Goals
1. Breathe together before the first note.
2. Each pick-up note should strengthen to beat 1 (downbeat).
3. Match articulation.
4. Match note lengths.
5. The wider the interval, the more focused the airstream should be.

Percussion Goals
1. Breathe together and start together.
2. Each pick-up note should strengthen to beat 1 (downbeat).
3. The quicker the notes, the smoother the mallet/stick motion should look.
4. Match the dynamic level of the winds.
5. Hands, wrists and arms should look natural and feel soft and relaxed.

5. Learning a Major Scale

Step 1   ## Step 2

Flute / Oboe

B♭ Clarinet / B♭ Bass Cl.

E♭ Alto Sax. / E♭ Bari. Sax. / E♭ Alto Cl.

B♭ Tenor Sax. / B♭ Trumpet / Baritone T.C.

F Horn

Trombone / Baritone / Bassoon / Elec. Bass / Tuba

*Mallet Instruments

Snare Drum / Bass Drum

Triangle / Tambourine

Timpani

Alternate Exercises   ### Alternate Exercises

B♭ Clarinet / B♭ Bass Cl.

F Horn

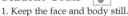 = Muffle (dampen)
*Xylophone, Bells, Marimba, Vibes
𝓟𝒆𝒅. (Vibes only)

Director Reminders
- Focus on the start and release of each note.
- Players should stay totally set during the rests, which are an active part of the phrase.
- A metronome will establish a steady pulse to help achieve all student goals.

Student Goals ✔
1. Keep the face and body still.
2. The tongue and fingers should move at exactly the same time.
3. Play the exercise in one breath.
4. Strive for a clear tone quality.
5. The embouchure should not move during rests.

Percussion Goals ✔
1. Breathe together and start together.
2. Strike the instrument in the same place with the same energy every time.
3. Posture should be natural with the body positions balanced.
4. Return the mallets/sticks to their starting position during rests and at the end of the exercise.
5. Hands, wrists and arms should look natural and feel soft and relaxed.

Step 3

Step 4

Director Reminders

- Focus on the start and release of each note.
- Players should stay totally set during the rests, which are an active part of the phrase.
- A metronome will establish a steady pulse to help achieve all student goals.

Student Goals ✓

1. Keep the face and body still.
2. The tongue and fingers should move at exactly the same time.
3. Play the exercise in one breath.
4. Strive for a clear tone quality.
5. The embouchure should not move during rests.

Percussion Goals ✓

1. Breathe together and start together.
2. Strike the instrument in the same place with the same energy every time.
3. Posture should be natural with the body positions balanced.
4. Return the mallets/sticks to their starting position during rests and at the end of the exercise.
5. Hands, wrists and arms should look natural and feel soft and relaxed.

Step 5

Student Goals ✓
1. Keep the face and body still.
2. The tongue and fingers should move at exactly the same time.
3. Play the exercise in one breath.
4. Strive for a clear tone quality.
5. The embouchure should not move during rests.

Percussion Goals ✓
1. Breathe together and start together.
2. Strike the instrument in the same place with the same energy every time.
3. Posture should be natural with the body positions balanced.
4. Return the mallets/sticks to their starting position during rests and at the end of the exercise.
5. Hands, wrists and arms should look natural and feel soft and relaxed.

6. Major Scale Exercises

6-1 Moving Down and Up (Tonguing and Slurring)

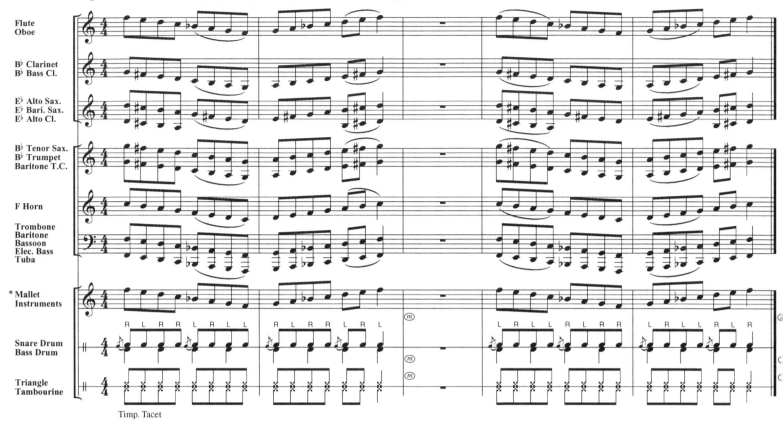

6-2 Moving Up and Down (Tonguing and Slurring)

Goals for Exercises 6-1 and 6-2

Director Reminders
- Review slurring technique with students.
- Players should stay totally set during the rests, which are an active part of the phrase.
- A metronome will establish a steady pulse to help achieve all student goals.

Student Goals ✓
1. Keep the air steady, constant and smooth.
2. Pay close attention to when notes are tongued or slurred.
3. All notes should have equal energy and volume.
4. Keep proper hand position while moving from note to note.
5. Play each scale in one breath.

Percussion Goals ✓
1. Breathe together and start together.
2. Strike the instrument in the same place with the same energy every time.
3. The quicker the notes, the smoother the mallet/stick motion should look.
4. Rolls should be smooth and even.
5. All flams should have the same quality of sound.

7. Learning a Chromatic Scale

7-1 Moving Up (6/8)
Step 1

Timp. Tacet

ⓜ = Muffle (dampen)
*Xylophone, Bells, Marimba, Vibes
🎹 (Vibes only)

Director Reminders
- Follow the process in Steps 1 and 2 to create a phrase when playing a chromatic scale.
- Review necessary notes and fingerings.
- A metronome will establish a steady pulse to help achieve all student goals.

Student Goals ✓
1. The tongue and fingers should move at exactly the same time.
2. Woodwinds should use special fingerings if suggested by your director.
3. Play the exercise in one breath.
4. Strive for a clear tone quality.
5. Each note should be equal in strength.

Percussion Goals ✓
1. Breathe together and start together.
2. Strike the instrument in the same place with the same energy every time.
3. Stroke beginnings should be smooth.
4. Hands, wrists and arms should look natural and feel soft and relaxed.
5. All flams should have the same quality of sound.

7-1 Moving Up (6/8)
Step 2

Timp. Tacet

Alternate Exercises

Director Reminders
- Follow the process in Steps 1 and 2 to create a phrase when playing a chromatic scale.
- Review necessary notes and fingerings.
- A metronome will establish a steady pulse to help achieve all student goals.

Student Goals
1. The tongue and fingers should move at exactly the same time.
2. Woodwinds should use special fingerings if suggested by your director.
3. Play the exercise in one breath.
4. Strive for a clear tone quality.
5. Each note should be equal in strength.

Percussion Goals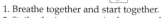
1. Breathe together and start together.
2. Strike the instrument in the same place with the same energy every time.
3. Stroke beginnings should be smooth.
4. Hands, wrists and arms should look natural and feel soft and relaxed.
5. All flams should have the same quality of sound.

7-1 Moving Up (6/8)
Step 3

Director Reminders
- Follow the process in Steps 1 and 2 to create a phrase when playing a chromatic scale.
- Review necessary notes and fingerings.
- A metronome will establish a steady pulse to help achieve all student goals.

Student Goals ✓
1. The tongue and fingers should move at exactly the same time.
2. Woodwinds should use special fingerings if suggested by your director.
3. Play the exercise in one breath.
4. Strive for a clear tone quality.
5. Each note should be equal in strength.

Percussion Goals ✓
1. Breathe together and start together.
2. Strike the instrument in the same place with the same energy every time.
3. Stroke beginnings should be smooth.
4. Hands, wrists and arms should look natural and feel soft and relaxed.
5. All flams should have the same quality of sound.

7-2 Moving Down
Step 1

Director Reminders
- Review necessary notes and fingerings.
- Players should stay totally set during the rests, which are an active part of the phrase.
- A metronome will establish a steady pulse to help achieve all student goals.

Student Goals
1. The tongue and fingers should move at exactly the same time.
2. Woodwinds should use special fingerings if suggested by your director.
3. Play the exercise in one breath.
4. Strive for a clear tone quality.
5. Each note should be equal in strength.

Percussion Goals
1. Breathe together and start together.
2. Strike the instrument in the same place with the same energy every time.
3. Stroke beginnings should be smooth.
4. Hands, wrists and arms should look natural and feel soft and relaxed.
5. All flams should have the same quality of sound.

Step 2

Director Reminders

- Review necessary notes and fingerings.
- Players should stay totally set during the rests, which are an active part of the phrase.
- A metronome will establish a steady pulse to help achieve all student goals.

Student Goals

1. The tongue and fingers should move at exactly the same time.
2. Woodwinds should use special fingerings if suggested by your director.
3. Play the exercise in one breath.
4. Strive for a clear tone quality.
5. Each note should be equal in strength.

Percussion Goals

1. Breathe together and start together.
2. Strike the instrument in the same place with the same energy every time.
3. Stroke beginnings should be smooth.
4. Hands, wrists and arms should look natural and feel soft and relaxed.
5. All flams should have the same quality of sound.

Step 3

Director Reminders

- Follow the process in Steps 1 and 2 to create a phrase when playing a chromatic scale.
- Players should stay totally set during the rests, which are an active part of the phrase.
- A metronome will establish a steady pulse to help achieve all student goals.

Student Goals

1. The tongue and fingers should move at exactly the same time.
2. Woodwinds should use special fingerings if suggested by your director.
3. Play the exercise in one breath.
4. Strive for a clear tone quality.
5. Each note should be equal in strength.

Percussion Goals

1. Breathe together and start together.
2. Strike the instrument in the same place with the same energy every time.
3. Stroke beginnings should be smooth.
4. Hands, wrists and arms should look natural and feel soft and relaxed.
5. All flams should have the same quality of sound.

7-3 Moving Up (4/4)
Step 1

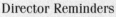

Director Reminders
- Review necessary notes and fingerings.
- Players should stay totally set during the rests, which are an active part of the phrase.
- A metronome will establish a steady pulse to help achieve all student goals.

Student Goals ✔
1. The tongue and fingers should move at exactly the same time.
2. Woodwinds should use special fingerings if suggested by your director.
3. Play the exercise in one breath.
4. Strive for a clear tone quality.
5. Each note should be equal in strength.

Percussion Goals ✔
1. Breathe together and start together.
2. Strike the instrument in the same place with the same energy every time.
3. Stroke beginnings should be smooth.
4. Hands, wrists and arms should look natural and feel soft and relaxed.
5. All flams should have the same quality of sound.

7-3 cont.
Step 2

Alternate Exercises

Director Reminders
- Review necessary notes and fingerings.
- Players should stay totally set during the rests, which are an active part of the phrase.
- A metronome will establish a steady pulse to help achieve all student goals.

Student Goals
1. The tongue and fingers should move at exactly the same time.
2. Woodwinds should use special fingerings if suggested by your director.
3. Play the exercise in one breath.
4. Strive for a clear tone quality.
5. Each note should be equal in strength.

Percussion Goals
1. Breathe together and start together.
2. Strike the instrument in the same place with the same energy every time.
3. Stroke beginnings should be smooth.
4. Hands, wrists and arms should look natural and feel soft and relaxed.
5. All flams should have the same quality of sound.

7-4 Moving Down
Step 1

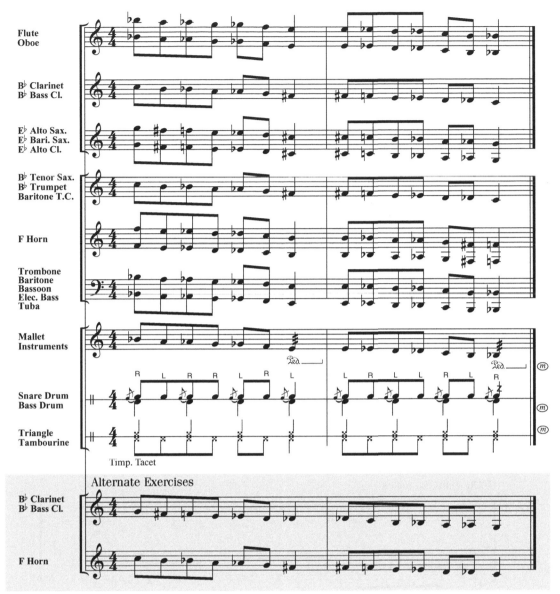

Director Reminders
- Review necessary notes and fingerings.
- Players should stay totally set during the rests, which are an active part of the phrase.
- A metronome will establish a steady pulse to help achieve all student goals.

Student Goals
1. The tongue and fingers should move at exactly the same time.
2. Woodwinds should use special fingerings if suggested by your director.
3. Play the exercise in one breath.
4. Strive for a clear tone quality.
5. Each note should be equal in strength.

Percussion Goals
1. Breathe together and start together.
2. Strike the instrument in the same place with the same energy every time.
3. Stroke beginnings should be smooth.
4. Hands, wrists and arms should look natural and feel soft and relaxed.
5. All flams should have the same quality of sound.

7-4 cont.
Step 2

Alternate Exercises

Director Reminders

- Review necessary notes and fingerings.
- Players should stay totally set during the rests, which are an active part of the phrase.
- A metronome will establish a steady pulse to help achieve all student goals.

Student Goals ✓

1. The tongue and fingers should move at exactly the same time.
2. Woodwinds should use special fingerings if suggested by your director.
3. Play the exercise in one breath.
4. Strive for a clear tone quality.
5. Each note should be equal in strength.

Percussion Goals ✓

1. Breathe together and start together.
2. Strike the instrument in the same place with the same energy every time.
3. Stroke beginnings should be smooth.
4. Hands, wrists and arms should look natural and feel soft and relaxed.
5. All flams should have the same quality of sound.

8. Chromatic Exercises in Fifths
8-1 Moving Down and Up

ⓜ = Muffle (dampen)
*Xylophone, Bells, Marimba, Vibes
🎵 (Vibes only)

Director Reminders
- Review necessary notes and fingerings.
- All intervals should resonate with the same character.
- A metronome will establish a steady pulse to help achieve all student goals.

Student Goals

1. Fingers must move at exactly the same time.
2. Keep the air steady, constant and smooth.
3. All notes should have equal energy and volume.
4. Keep the airstream focused.
5. During quarter rests, breathe on count 4.

Percussion Goals
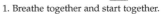
1. Breathe together and start together.
2. Posture should be natural with the body position balanced.
3. Match the dynamic level of the winds.
4. Triangle and tambourine each should have a consistent quality of sound, note-to-note.
5. All flams should have the same quality of sound.

8-2 Moving Up and Down

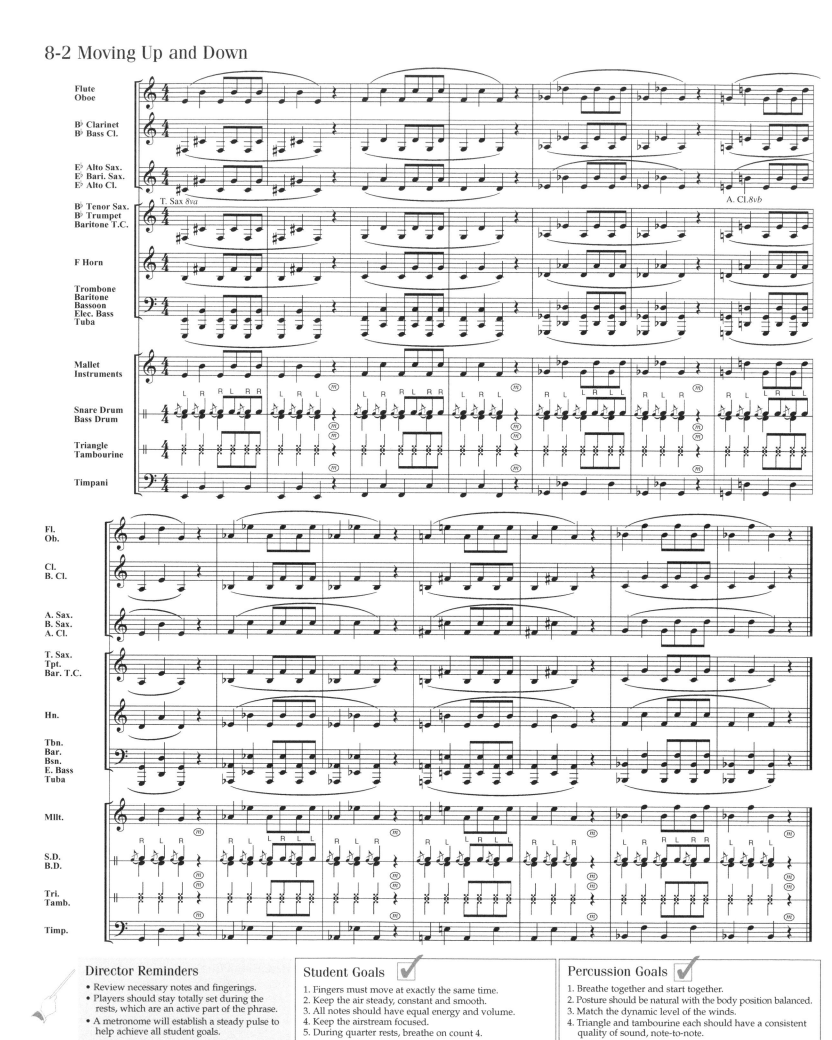

Director Reminders
- Review necessary notes and fingerings.
- Players should stay totally set during the rests, which are an active part of the phrase.
- A metronome will establish a steady pulse to help achieve all student goals.

Student Goals ✓
1. Fingers must move at exactly the same time.
2. Keep the air steady, constant and smooth.
3. All notes should have equal energy and volume.
4. Keep the airstream focused.
5. During quarter rests, breathe on count 4.

Percussion Goals ✓
1. Breathe together and start together.
2. Posture should be natural with the body position balanced.
3. Match the dynamic level of the winds.
4. Triangle and tambourine each should have a consistent quality of sound, note-to-note.
5. All flams should have the same quality of sound.

9. Rhythm and Tonguing Exercises with Triplets

9-1 Long to Short Notes

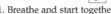

(m) = Muffle (dampen)
*Xylophone, Bells, Marimba, Vibes
Ped. (Vibes only)

Director Reminders
- Focus on the front of each note for accuracy and consistency.
- Players should stay totally set during the rests, which are an active part of the phrase.
- A metronome will establish a steady pulse to help achieve all student goals.

Student Goals ✓
1. Breathe and start together.
2. The tongue should move up and down naturally; the same part of the tongue should go to the same spot with the same strength each time.
3. Match articulation.
4. Match note lengths.
5. Keep the air steady, constant and smooth.

Percussion Goals ✓
1. Breathe together and start together.
2. Dampen to match the end of the wind players' notes.
3. Match the dynamic level of the winds.
4. Strike the instrument in the same place with the same energy every time.
5. The hand, wrist and arm motion should look the same hand-to-hand.

9-2 Short to Long Notes

Director Reminders
- Focus on the front of each note for accuracy and consistency.
- Players should stay totally set during the rests, which are an active part of the phrase.
- A metronome will establish a steady pulse to help achieve all student goals.

Student Goals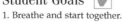
1. Breathe and start together.
2. The tongue should move up and down naturally; the same part of the tongue should go to the same spot with the same strength each time.
3. Match articulation.
4. Match note lengths.
5. Keep the air steady, constant and smooth.

Percussion Goals
1. Breathe together and start together.
2. Dampen to match the end of the wind players' notes.
3. Match the dynamic level of the winds.
4. Strike the instrument in the same place with the same energy every time.
5. The hand, wrist and arm motion should look the same hand-to-hand.

10. Combining Eighth and Sixteenth Notes

Variation 1

ⓜ = Muffle (dampen)
*Xylophone, Bells, Marimba, Vibes
𝄞 (Vibes only)

Director Reminders
- Focus on the front of each note for accuracy and consistency.
- Players should stay totally set during the rests, which are an active part of the phrase.
- A metronome will establish a steady pulse to help achieve all student goals.

Student Goals
1. The face should feel natural and the texture of the lips should be soft.
2. The tongue should move up and down naturally; the same part of the tongue should go to the same spot with the same strength each time.
3. Articulation should not weaken as rhythms become more active.
4. Keep the air steady, constant and smooth.
5. As notes get quicker, more air should move down the center of the instrument.

Percussion Goals
1. Breathe together and start together.
2. The quicker the notes, the smoother the mallet/stick motion should look.
3. Rolls should be smooth and even.
4. Strike the instrument in the same place with the same energy every time.
5. Posture should be natural with the body position balanced.

Variation 2

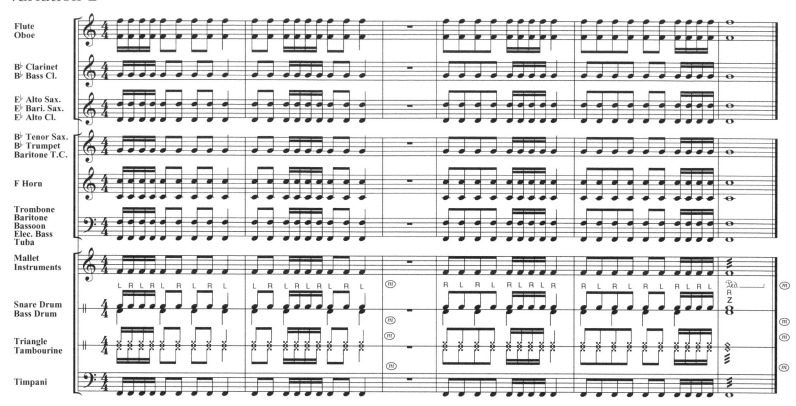

Variation 3

Director Reminders

- Focus on the front of each note for accuracy and consistency.
- In Variation 4, players should stay totally set during the rests, which are an active part of the phrase.
- A metronome will establish a steady pulse to help achieve all student goals.

Student Goals ✓

1. The face should feel natural and the texture of the lips should be soft.
2. The tongue should move up and down naturally; the same part of the tongue should go to the same spot with the same strength each time.
3. Strive for a clear tone quality.
4. Keep the air steady, constant and smooth.
5. Each note should be equal in strength.

Percussion Goals ✓

1. Breathe together and start together.
2. The quicker the notes, the smoother the mallet/stick motion should look.
3. Rolls should be smooth and even.
4. Strike the instrument in the same place with the same energy every time.
5. Posture should be natural with the body position balanced.

Variation 4

Variation 5

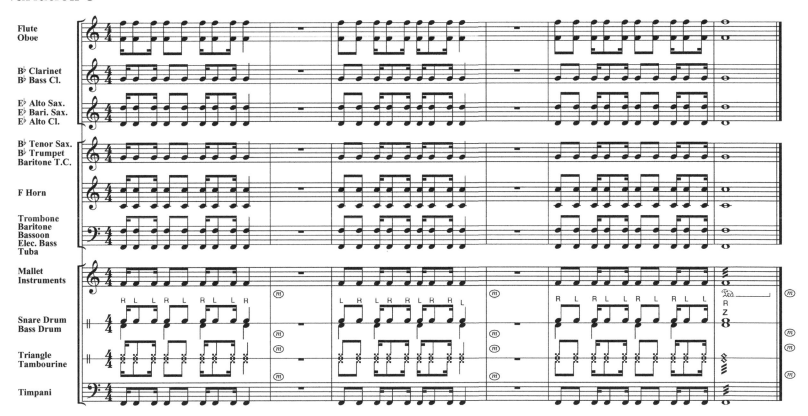

Director Reminders

- Focus on the front of each note for accuracy and consistency.
- Players should stay totally set during the rests, which are an active part of the phrase.
- A metronome will establish a steady pulse to help achieve all student goals.

Student Goals

1. The face should feel natural and the texture of the lips should be soft.
2. The tongue should move up and down naturally; the same part of the tongue should go to the same spot with the same strength each time.
3. Strive for a clear tone quality.
4. Keep the air steady, constant and smooth.
5. Each note should be equal in strength.

Percussion Goals

1. Breathe together and start together.
2. The quicker the notes, the smoother the mallet/stick motion should look.
3. Rolls should be smooth and even.
4. Strike the instrument in the same place with the same energy every time.
5. Posture should be natural with the body position balanced.

Variation 6

Director Reminders

- Focus on the front of each note for accuracy and consistency.
- Players should stay totally set during the rests, which are an active part of the phrase.
- A metronome will establish a steady pulse to help achieve all student goals.

Student Goals

1. Always think three sixteenth notes inside of each dotted eighth note.
2. The tongue should move up and down naturally; the same part of the tongue should go to the same spot with the same strength each time.
3. Strive for a clear tone quality.
4. Keep the air steady, constant and smooth.
5. The face should feel natural and the texture of the lips should be soft.

Percussion Goals

1. Breathe together and start together.
2. The quicker the notes, the smoother the mallet/stick motion should look.
3. Rolls should be smooth and even.
4. Strike the instrument in the same place with the same energy every time.
5. Posture should be natural with the body position balanced.

Posture

Introducing a natural approach to body position and posture will allow students to breath correctly. As students progress through a band program, correct playing posture is often ignored. The success of the ensemble is directly related to the diligent attention to this type of detail. Ask yourself: "Would I use my students as role models for an example of excellent posture?" The various aspects of correct posture should be recognized and reinforced daily. Using the steps listed below, teach correct standing posture before sitting.

Standing Posture

The body should feel balanced and flexible. With feet slightly more than shoulder width apart, shoulders are sloping and in line with the feet and hips. The head is balanced in the middle of the shoulders (floating in place), and the rib cage is lifted with the bottom two ribs floating.

Sitting Posture

- The "sit-as-you-stand" concept is vital.
- Correct posture should be addressed early in the class period.
- The design of the chair should not influence correct posture.
- Not all chairs within a section have to be at the same angle (especially for flutes and French horns).
- Where the student sits on the chair is not as important as the balance of the body (determined by the length of the student's legs and instrument size).
- A student should be able to stand up and walk naturally directly from their "seated position."
- The feet should be naturally apart, the same width as when standing.
- Students should keep their feet "soft" so their toes do not curl inside their shoes.

Using a Music Stand

The music stand should be positioned directly in front of the student, with one spoke facing the student. The stand should be high enough for the students to see both the music and conductor with ease. Students can tap their feet on either side of the spoke.

Breathing

After correct posture is established, it is time to incorporate breathing: the foundation of all wind playing. In this book, breathing is addressed from the viewpoint of the ensemble. While there are many similarities to breathing as individuals, the practice of breathing as an ensemble has it's own set of objectives that directly affect the foundation of ensemble playing. The following ideas provide ways to rehearse ensemble breathing, while making players aware of the breathing process and it's affect on making music.

- Breathing should be a natural process, with the face still, and no upper body movement in response to the air taken in.
- Daily breathing exercises will help calm players.
- The air is always moving in or out, like waves – it never stops.
- In order to get the maximum air intake, breathe through the mouth.
- There should be no unnatural creases in the face when playing.
- Keep the eyes soft and open, and eyebrows apart.
- The shape of the mouth should be natural and does not change.
- All breathing activity should be below the rib cage.
- The tongue should be in its natural position, physically soft, but not touching the lower teeth and gums.
- When air is taken in, it should feel cool on the tongue – if it doesn't, the tongue is too far back in the mouth.
- The temperature of exhaled air is determined by the vowel sound the player emulates. The taller the vowel shape inside the mouth, the warmer the air will be. This can greatly affect the resonance of tone quality.
- There should be no extraneous noise when breathing correctly.
- Let air in and out naturally, as opposed to "sucking in."
- The diaphragm will expand naturally – very little information is needed – it is an involuntary muscle.
- The body responds to the air – rather than controlling it.
- When there is a pulse, players should learn to gauge how much air they need considering the phrase and tempo.
- When breathing exercises are mastered with a natural face, embouchure formation can be added with special attention to the placement of the corners of the mouth.
- The position of the tongue should stay the same in all breathing exercises. It should be controlled only by the vowel sound emulated. The conductor should designate specific vowel sounds for each instrument and breathing exercise.
- To successfully create resonant sounds, the air should resonate in the body and travel past the embouchure.

Articulation Basics

- The tongue should be used as naturally as when speaking, moving up and down – not back and forth.

- Within a given style, the tongue touches the same spot with the same strength every time.

- The air should be focused to the center – and strong enough to support the tongue's natural movement.

- The smaller the note value the firmer the strength of articulation.

- Within a chosen musical passage, the articulation should not be affected by the duration of the note.

- To create an illusion of sameness, the student may have to articulate "firmer as they go" when playing repeated segments/patterns.

- Do not interpret legato articulation as an opportunity to move the tongue down slowly – the more legato that is desired, the quicker the tongue should move, so the air is not interrupted.

- The speed of the rhythm within the tempo of the music does not relate to the speed with which the tongue moves down.

- Brass players' tongues can move to more than one place on the teeth for particular registers, while woodwind players' tongues always touch in the same spot.

- Watch all parts of a student's face when articulating. The embouchure should never be involved in the articulation process; only the air and tongue should move when a student is articulating.

- Articulation should in no way affect the resonance or release of a note.

- The faster the articulation, the more air should be placed in the center of the instrument, past the embouchure.

- No sound is ever stopped with the tongue unless it is used as a special effect.

- When articulating correctly, the tongue is in its "down" position much longer than in the "up" position.

- It is possible to create different sounds on brass instruments by changing the vowel sounds along with the articulation. Woodwind instruments basically use the same vowel sound throughout.

- It is perfectly acceptable to hold the jaw still with a hand while vocalizing an articulated syllable – instruments should be placed in a safe place when doing this.

- When the students vocalize an articulation, they should form the corners of the mouth as they would for their embouchure – corners may be held in place with the index and middle finger.

- The students should understand that focusing the articulation is as important as focusing their sound.

- When articulating, the air should be mentally placed in the same spot in the room for every note.
- If it's possible to have "like" instrument sectionals, check the students' articulation skills by having them articulate on their mouthpiece/mouthpiece and barrel/mouthpiece and neck and head joint. Double reeds may use their instruments when working on articulation basics. Articulation difficulties can be exposed by practicing in this manner – even with high school players. Often the instrument will "mask" problems that will be obvious with mouthpieces alone.
- If the brass players use a thumb and two fingers on their mouthpiece, watch for the natural slant as it would appear if they were using their instruments.
- Often articulation is the determining factor in the effect of the musical line. It serves no purpose to articulate beautifully if the fingers are not coordinated with the tongue.

Balance Essentials

Balance should be treated as "layers" of color, not just numerous colors blended together. Adopting this approach will allow various combinations of timbres to create many desirable effects.

Dynamics should be relative from section to section. If the entire ensemble has a written f, adjust the volume from instrument to instrument, depending on each instrument's place in the harmonic series, with the goal of creating a unified ensemble f.

Balance involves matching:
- Tonal energy
- Articulation
- Releases
- Rhythmic movement

Other balance considerations:
- Tessitura (such as a piccolo trying to play "soft" in the upper register)
- Instruments in octaves (the lower octave should support the upper octave)
- Texture (color instruments, such as double reeds and horn, need to be heard)

Conducting

The conductor's role is to describe the intent of the score using terminology the students can understand, in order to recreate the music in performance. The actual baton technique used should reflect the aural result of this learning process.

Ask yourself:

- Do I count or sing along with my ensemble – instead of listening to them play?
- Is my posture as natural and balanced as the posture of my students?
- Am I conducting with gestures that are clear and concise for the age group of my students?
- Do I hear how my students actually sound as opposed to how I would like them to sound?
- Is my conducting a distraction to the listener?
- Does my conducting reflect the music?
- Am I conducting what I see on the score?
- Is my body language surpassing the musical experience of my students?
- If I were listening to my group, would I be bored or distracted?
- Am I relating concepts to my students drawn from age-appropriate experiences?
- Do I recognize what skills are needed to perform a selected piece successfully with my ensemble?

Essential Playing Concepts

Watch for:

- Upper bodies that look the same sitting as standing.
- Natural looking faces. Have students check the look of their face in a mirror. They should remember how it feels when playing.
- A natural looking shoulder area.
- Soft (relaxed) palms and elbows, and natural "flat C" hand positions.
- Wrists that are not lower than the palm of the hand.
- Feet always in place so the student can rise out of the chair without extra movement.
- Chairs that allow students to sit with proper posture based on their individual height.
- Ribcages that are "lifted" off the stomach.
- Backs appearing to move slightly towards the stomach, to balance the upper body in the chair.
- Upper arms not pressed against the chest.
- Balanced, "floating" heads centered on the shoulders
- Feet that are not behind the knees and shoulders.
- Complete stillness in the upper body above the bottom ribs, and no change of facial expression.
- Corners of the mouth move in or down toward the center of the embouchure – never out or up.
- Stillness in the face when articulating.
- Faces appear natural, no matter what register the student is playing.

- Brass players not pivoting while playing.
- Brass instrument mouthpieces slant slightly down from the mouth.
- The red flesh on the outside of the mouthpieces not tense or stretched.
- Unnecessary body motion when playing (i.e., raised shoulders, leaning forward at the waist, etc.) – extra motion will affect the air stream.

Listen for:

- No extra noises in the room, other than the sounds of the instruments, creating a calm quiet atmosphere during instruction and quiet musical passages.
- No extraneous noises when air is taken into the body, and no hesitation of air as it returns to the instrument.
- No extraneous noises at the beginnings or ends (open-throat release) of notes.
- Controlled air that is constant, steady, smooth and at the velocity to create the student's most resonant sound.
- The matching of tonal energy and color when moving from one note to the next, regardless of intervallic distance.
- With touching notes, match the air at the end of the first note with the beginning of the next note.
- No change in the tonal color when playing outside of the instrument's normal "mid-range."
- No interruption of sounds caused by fingers moving unnaturally and inaccurately, or not being coordinated with articulations.
- Notes on weak beats are often neglected, but in reality, lead the music forward.
- The end of each note before a rest should be as clean as the start of each note.
- Balancing from side to side within a section, and from front to back.
- The last note in each measure and first note of the following measure sounding the same in regards to tonal energy, tonal color, tonal strength and articulation.
- Articulation, judged by how the front of each note sounds.
- Style, judged by how the back of each note sounds.
- Articulated passages, regardless of rhythmic value, articulated with the same strength (the smaller the note value, the firmer the articulation).
- The vowel sound not changing when releasing a note.
- Releases that aren't created by stopping the air with the tongue or closing the embouchure.
- Releases that do not change the pitch as a result of physical or air-related changes.
- Students "fitting into" what is already going on (whether they re-enter as the dominant or secondary interest).
- The full ensemble sounding as clean and tonally pure as the model.
- A particular sound that is the "foundation" for the color.
- The brass sound to be as vibrant as the woodwinds.
- A new style should be obvious to the listener from the first note.
- Each pick-up note should be as firmly articulated as the first downbeat note.

Additional Ensemble Concepts

- The illusion of dynamic contrast and/or effect can be created by using the proper balance of the harmonic series.

- The mechanical tuner should be used only when establishing a pitch center for the ensemble (i.e., in relation to A-440). It should not be used for linear or vertical interval tuning, except for the octave and the perfect fifth. All other intervals are played in relation to the key center of the music. Students should be discouraged from using individual tuners at their stands when playing in the ensemble. They should be taught to play in relation to those around them.

- Regardless of the tonal maturity of the group, students should never be allowed to play beyond their instruments' most resonant sound. This happens when there is extraneous noise in their sound.

- Practice very fast music slowly, and practice very slow music faster than marked. Then, gradually work towards the desired tempo. Learn every new piece within the abilities and/or limitations of individual student skills. Allow students time to think and react to the skills needed to play the music chosen.

- Teach students to vocalize rhythm and pulse. When dealing with rhythms within an ensemble, it is better to think of rhythms by the number of beamed notes. Instead of using a counting system, it is sometimes more effective to utilize a succession of numbers. For example, rather than counting four sixteenth notes as "1-ee-and-ah" or "1-ta-te-ta," have students count "1-2-3-4." Counting by numbers gives a better sense of what is happening in the beam; it keeps technique from slowing down and forces them to articulate clearly by the use of consonants. When vocalizing, the corners of the mouth should be in position as when creating the embouchure. Think of the counting sound as supported and vocally centered, similar to an articulated passage when played on the instrument. Vocalization expectations should be the same as when playing – confident, aggressive, articulate, focused, centered, supported, etc.

- Clapping rhythms can create a stable infrastructure for the overall rhythmic scheme. The following procedure is used:
  a. One hand and arm should remain stationary – it does not matter which.
  b. The other hand claps the rhythm and remains close to the stationary hand – faster rhythms are impossible if the clapping hand is too far away.
  c. Make sure that the clapping hand strikes the stationary hand with the same strength as the articulation.
  d. Make sure that both hands keep the same shape at all times.
  e. The volume of the clapping should not interfere with the clarity of the rhythm and/or combined rhythms.
  f. Teach students to listen for their rhythmic line in relation to others in the room.
  g. Teach students to be sensitive, and not to interfere with the basic rhythmic structure as their part enters and exits the texture.